Presented to

Katie Clapp

St Thomas's

Sunday School

Doxey

11. 7. 1993

CHRISTIAN ART LTD, EXETER, 0392 77277

NOTE TO PARENTS

This familiar Bible story has been retold in a sensitive and simple way so that young children can read and understand it for themselves. But the special message of the story remains unchanged. It is the message of God's love and care for us all.

Daniel in the Lions' Den

retold by Marjorie Newman
illustrated by Edgar Hodges

Copyright © 1990 World International Publishing Ltd.
All rights reserved.
Published in Great Britain by World International Publishing Ltd.,
an Egmont Company, Egmont House, PO Box 111, Great Ducie Street,
Manchester M60 3BL.
Printed in Germany.
ISBN 0 7235 4466 2
Reprinted 1992

A catalogue record for this book is available from the British Library

Daniel lived in Jerusalem, in the Bible lands. One day Nebuchadnezzar, the king of Babylon, attacked the city.

His armies captured many people. They were carried off to Babylon. Among the prisoners were Daniel and three of his friends. It was very frightening. But Daniel knew God would be with him.

"All the boys from Jerusalem are to have special food," ordered Nebuchadnezzar. "And they are to have special training. After three years I shall choose the best ones to serve me." But Daniel would not eat the rich food.

Bravely he said to the guard, "Please give us plain food." In the end, the guard agreed. Daniel and his friends grew very fit. And God made them wise.

After three years Nebuchadnezzar sent for them. Nebuchadnezzar asked them hard questions. They answered ten times as well as his own wise men! He chose them to serve him.

Years went by. Now Darius, king of the Medes and Persians, had captured Babylon. He needed someone to be chief ruler there. He chose Daniel.

The other rulers were furious. "We must get rid of Daniel!" They plotted jealously.

The rulers soon made a plan. They knew that Daniel prayed every day to God . . .

They went to Darius. "O King," they bowed, "you should make a new law. For thirty days people must pray only to you. If anyone disobeys, he must be thrown to the lions!"

Darius listened. Pray to *him*? He *must* be a great king. "Very well," he smiled. "I will make the law."

"Write down the law at once!" urged the rulers. They held their breath . . . But once more, Darius agreed. Now the law could never be altered! Gleefully, the rulers made it known to everyone.

When Daniel heard it, he knew a trap had been set. He must either give up his daily prayers to God – or be thrown to the lions. His enemies would be watching . . .

Daniel made up his mind. He would go on praying to God. He went to his upstairs room. He stood by the windows which faced towards Jerusalem, and he prayed to God to help him.

His enemies knew their plot had worked.

Gleefully, the rulers rushed to the king. "King Darius, live for ever!" they bowed. "Did you not make a law saying that for thirty days people must pray only to you?"

"Yes, I did," agreed Darius, puzzled.

"Daniel still prays to his God!" they said. Then *Darius* saw the trap which had been set. He was very upset. Daniel was a favourite of his. All day the king tried to find a way to save him.

But it was no use. Sadly, the king ordered that Daniel be brought to the lions' den. "Daniel," he said, "may the God whom you serve so faithfully keep you safe!" Then Daniel was thrown to the lions.

A stone was rolled across the mouth of the den. King Darius had to seal it with his own ring. Now everyone would know if the stone was moved. There was no chance of rescuing Daniel.

King Darius went back to the palace. But he couldn't eat. He lay down. He couldn't sleep. All night he thought about Daniel.

At the first light of dawn Darius got up. He hurried back to the lions' den. He was full of fear. Had Daniel been torn to pieces?

As soon as Darius was close to the den he called out. "Daniel! Has your God saved you?" Trembling, he waited.

And Daniel's voice answered, strong and clear. "O King, I am safe. God did not let the lions harm me!"

King Darius was overjoyed. "Get Daniel out!" he shouted.

The men who had thrown Daniel in, lifted him out. They couldn't *believe* it! He was completely unhurt.

Then the king called, "Let Daniel's accusers be brought here. *They* shall be thrown to the lions!"

So the rulers were thrown into the lions' den. And the lions killed them before they even touched the ground.

And King Darius wrote, "This is my order. Everyone shall show respect for Daniel's God. For truly his God is great, and will last for ever."